PETREA SAVIGE

WAITING FOR ANGELS

Littlefox Press

WAITING FOR ANGELS
Petrea Savige

Published by Littlefox Press
PO Box 816
Kyneton VIC 3444

ISBN 978-0-9925562-8-0

In memory of

Sandy Shively

❧ BOOK ONE ❧

WAITING FOR ANGELS

A new mythology

THE CHARACTERS

The Mother of Eve: *Eve's mother*
Eve: *the first woman*
Adam: *Eve's husband*
Cain: *Eve's eldest son*
Abel: *Eve's second son and Judassa's twin brother*
Judassa: *Eve's only daughter and Abel's twin sister*

CONTENTS

MOTHER AND CHILD

I am filled by two desires

to hold you forever
to liberate you with nobility

and suppose I will thread
some jagged line between them.

This seems to me the sacred thought

in our holding and our letting go
we are the great practitioners of love

saying gladly at every Fall

this is my body and blood
which shall be given up for you.

FOR THE LOVE OF GODS
To my Husband

Though you are Mars and fiery
bull-headed, strong like ox
but also passionate, tender
moved readily

though you do not live in air
but time
devour it
remind each minute of its passing

though you broke the very rocks
with your bare hands
took your heart from fires
and leapt up in the air
with the earth still in your hair
to find me

though you are come
like a great bird through the dark
to bring me back

this time I must tell it
from outside the stars and looking down.

PART ONE

MOTHER OF EVE

The wind howls tonight
hisses in my ear,
Eve's dead
and Judassa's gone
like some small ghost alone.

I suppose traditions
must begin clumsily,
a kiss to mark the victim.

Shift one piece
drops and locks
the mind hammers.

Find the step at the bottom
take aside the leaves
the beetles scatter.

Claw of pen and a mind full of hooks.
Where to begin?

I am old

indiscretion runs down my chin.
I am old.
I rummage through bags late at night
you think I'm mad.

I am old.
I sit on the quiet seats of town
and in the stillness of the bricks
and the road and the hills
you do not see me.

I hear the comings and the goings
doors opening and closing
the footsteps.

I sit on the seats, in the doorways
by the bridges, by the sweating parks
and glittering cities

and hear the roaring
the coming and the going
the lives and lives and lives
the avalanche of you.

Can it be imagined?

Another story.

Out of the mists
along paths

can it be imagined
a people
and an ancient time.

Before.

Out of the mists
(picture it
moss paws on rocks)

out of the white mists
from the reeds
from the edge

of light on water of lake

paths
tracks

walking across earth.
What atmosphere
what fear

to see
coming from afar

another.
Watching the approach
step by step
assessing the circumstances.

Alone
and a meeting
at the crossing of paths.

Interconnectedness of stones.
Interconnectedness of bones.

After a reading of Kenneth Clark's Civilization

What's left? you said.
What's left out you mean I said.

Civilization is what is enduring, beautiful, universal

and you hardly mentioned me
and were not once surprised by my absence.

The greatest ages have been and gone you say
you are not sure what comes next
perhaps a new Dark Age.

I am graceless, unlovely
I am also enduring, beautiful, universal
and I have pity, mercy, forgiveness
in my fashion

as well as rage, hatred
desire for revenge.
In my fashion.

Looking for Paradise

Where should I look?

Isis went looking
for the pieces of her husband
put him back together
and they worshipped him
for a thousand years.

They found the statue of King Cheops
upside down in a well.
Used rocks from one pyramid
for their own next attempt
at immortality.

The other woman gave a son.
Had him given back
bloody and broken.

Ancient woman
filed her nails on soapstone
for a fine edge.

They found her bones.

I have stood at windows

in old houses
and wondered at the lives
from inside there.

Who listened on the worn out stair.

I have wondered
at the lives lived
in the kitchens
at the hearths
behind the curtains.

The point of view from the window seat.
The dreaming done at the fire.

Lives lived so quietly
in time with the TV programs
and the meals.

Something to look forward to.
Something lovely to believe in.

Touch a crumb
from cloth to lip.

Sigh and reach
for one more piece of cake.

I have heard of them

tortured
shut up and left to starve

whipped for having bodies that were loving

left to give birth
out under the sky. Alone.

Perhaps those in charge of death
have lost the fear of it
blooded like dogs.

Poor cow.
The blood runs down from the abattoir.
The smell, the knowledge is certain
the sacrifice is meaningless.

It is all lost now
(the clean stone, the knife prepared)

All is known now. Seen. Set free.

No more slow dancing
at the secret door of the unknown garden.

We scatter like leaves
are wary of the moon.

You think you cannot change

have metamorphosed into rock
set brittle
hard.

I fear loneliness.

In the present continuous
of children playing
of someone being beaten
cannot forget
the quickening within me

primary division
first leaf.

Cannot forget the faces of the children
sleeping in the street. Alone.

Freeing the mind
is like freeing a wild cat
all angles appear at once.

I am wandering wide
like a bagwoman under a bridge
forgotten how to go home.

PART TWO

EVE SHE

In the great tearing of you from me
there was to be
such new life.

Divided against ourselves
split in two
a long time ago.

Ancient crags of mind begin to move.

Voices older than this
hid in the rocks at Delphi

spoke in the thunder
in the whisper of trees.

There I am at Ankora
giving birth between two leopards.

Leopards and pomegranates!
My combs and pins
my water mirror.

In those days I had style.
Somewhat a museum piece now.

Perfection has its own devices

its own price. In seeking forgiveness, in forgiving
eternal giving, purest forms, we learned to hate,
to judge, to condemn ourselves
to be born again instead of born of woman.

My daughter Eve was taken.
It was for the best, they said.

She was to be kept away
in a place that had it all.
I was to say nothing,

all would be revealed.

An experiment
to split good from evil
the spirit from the body,

some distillation.

Rent-free for life
in a divine place.

I said to mind the small print.

Apple eating

Eve, smiling,
finished the apple
tossed the core.

Prodigal daughters
sinned originally
in their own style.

Are they well shriven?
Forgiven?

The fatted calf I wonder
or the whip?

And cast her down
and sloughed her like a skin.

Denied in this Divinity, Delight

took a God from elsewhere
by a Virgin pure and simple,
so beautiful, so squeaky clean
the painters dreamed new faces
for eternity.

The Fall they called it

She'd fallen alright.

I saw the light begin in her hair, her skin
could see it in her face in days
and waited for her
longed for her to say

but what?

She had no words.

To fall, to sin, to know, to be known.

To find out in terror.

My dearest daughter.

Began to hide herself from me

would not look at me.

I was full of things to tell her
she was frightened, denying, full of secrets.

And the wall went up
and she went over in her rage
like a fire.

Disappeared in flowers and incense
and almost did not get back.

I followed at my pace
and waited for her time to come.

The first labour was hers

split her like a rock
spilt her with pain

until that great mothering cry
and she took the baby to her
and forgot it all.

Ancient meridians of touch.
I had no fear it would revive itself
the gentleness, fierce power of tenderness
the tiny thing.
Power of the human baby born.

Nice symbol.
Taken out of our hands.

Out of the context of the will,
the urgency,
the great surge
to life.

I saw her before the twins Abel and Judassa
huge, wanton, generous, lovely
sat in the shade with a plateful of peaches
catching the fruit as it fell.

They could not conceive,
could not believe
that the mystery was part of
so vile, so beautiful a thing as woman.

Guilt is an oil slick

She studied jealousy carefully
saw the hollowness begin.

And suddenly one day
there it was
clear as a dream
the one above ready to drop
the one in the furrow with a killing look
and the crack of bone on bone.

She made to scream
no sound
he smiles.

Ashes explode and float
are the whisperings in the skull of an old man
who cannot pray and cannot sleep.

Bright gold flies
sip at the dead man's eyes.

Dear Abel.

We buried him
and then began
some kind of dark age of the heart.

To forget a sin

it's different from forgive.

If I could have found one word to say

release her

but she was well beyond my power
and lived like there was always more to pay.

I held her
she was easy as a child
but hardly saw me
looked far beyond me
well past tears

and begged me
give her something.
To finish.

Begged me.
and I gave it.

Now two ghosts walk in me.

She was a woman at nine

and she knew it
like a bird knows how to fly.

I must believe
she was curious, brave, wise, mysterious
a woman in her loving
as eager and delighted
as the rest of us.

I alone believe in her sacredness

and will raise altars
and keep lights burning.

I thought to join the ranks of the great avengers

but it was not like that at all.

Nothing touches me.

Things slide over and by.

I am walking with her
deadly

do not try to contact me.

The cold wind of centuries
springs at the window
the season
suddenly closes.

Fungus and cobwebs over us all.

PART THREE

JUDASSA ALONE

Inquisition as Metaphor

At Avilla the wind is still cold
the land still
dead in the rain shadow.

Out of the dark night
we were split like timber
rode through the streets
the mob
burning
shrieking
mad for
purity
flings us
(before our children's eyes)
spills us
like a waterfall
into a thousand light years
of pure tears.

The screams go on till daybreak.

London Underground

We descend.

Lights flicker and crack
beneath the moving stair
down, down into the warm thick air.

This must be the promised place
we hang and sway
our faces white
through the black roaring of tunnels.

No one speaks
and no one looks too long.

Silence.

The doors are shut.

We are taken into darkness.

They take from you with ragged hands
what you didn't want to give

they hook you with eyes.

The lights go down
and the darkness blinds you for a while
until the sun rises
on you alone there
formless
until you take shape
and ride all over them
with promises, promises
of much much more
until you have them eating out of your hand.

You are winking, prismatic, lovelier
than all their dreams
turning tricks, ready if called upon
sympathetic, tender
quick-change emotions
until you are one dimensional
holograph on a cloud.

They want to hold you in a freeze frame
catch the spinning, tearing light of you.

Rewind you, replay you at leisure.

At the Paradise Hotel

This is the moment now.
We are alone
caught out of time
in that long still pause
before the lift door opens

the heavy door
that takes you to the bare room
with the hanging light over the bed
and single straight-backed chair.

Towels provided
no breakfast.

A wayside stop.
The anonymity of a road.

This is the place

the land between two borders.

Nowhere.

She has removed all sign posts
as an act of hostility
(a cleverness also she thought)
There is no way out.

She is escaping,
watching,
stalking herself with a sniper's eye
accurate
and no pity.

She lies hidden in compartments
flattened into segments
separated by walls
enclosed in the rubble
far down in the bunker

hears the whisperings above

is outside our range.

Sound the alarm,
she panics and starts

she is brittle
and jumps at shadows

but cunning.
Eyes behind the glass
behind the mirrors
and double mirrors
trickery and secrets
for watching unobserved

she has learned all these
and spies at leisure
at moments of unconsciousness
at cracks in the wall
making notes.

Do not approach:
She will shatter
splinter into dangerous pieces.

They pierce her heart.

Postcard One

I saw Donatello's Magdalene
and thought the very life
was gone from her.

Someone understood.

Another kind of war had taken place in her
and she had lost.

Postcard Two

I saw black angels with green hair.
Dark and sullen
they stood vigil at a bombed cathedral
drank cheap wine
and guarded their places by the wall with dogs.

A jittery peace at best
a temporary cease-fire only.

The siren's wailing still fills me with despair.

Guided Tour

You will see that
after the golden halo left the picture
the light came from without.

The human form became solid
and changes shape
and must be dealt with.

It was a day of beauty and the trees shone.
The sun, a more delicate, watery affair
comes through windows
onto walls
lights faces from above
touching cheeks
flowers, leaves
the straw hats of women
the hand of the artist.

For a time the world shimmered and flickered
like a vision.

Soon the forms themselves slid off the paper

angular
divided
nothing certain.

Change Room Public Baths

Turned suddenly

felt someone move
behind the steaming air.

Stopped.

Moved again.

As she did
so the other.

Saw
a gold softness
shocked
a loveliness of skin
parabola of belly
glittering, descending.

Moved again
in sudden fear
held out her hands to pass

and touched the glass.

The mirror of herself first laughed
then cried in love.

Semi-formal: the Dream Feeders

Powder dusk
a dry white rind of moon.
Flowers spill their perfume
and the slow haze sets over us.

Decisions must be made,
arrange the lamps.

A bal masqué is easiest don't you think
for the unmasking, the playfulness
for the wearing of capes and shawls
for dressing up mysterious eyes.

The late places are few and known to few
all night and never day really.

Violins are water and trembling leaves.

The dawn is stark crimson.

Only the poor blind bat trusts the dark,
survives stealing from the night's sleeping pockets.
A damp and black-winged figure
scrambles towards the west.

Judassa Touriste

rides on her bicycle
down through the trees
the shadows glide over her,
tumbles out
through the small town
to the beach on a warm afternoon,
quiet thoughts together
bodies resting.

Children squeal and scurry in the shallows
wooden gulls glide under clouds
and an ancient sun glitters undefeated.

At the dewpoint of the soul
returns to earth
lodestone of the heart.

Black dog laughing on brown sand under blue sky
with white time clocks.

Pick one
sense the instant

slip into the present
then truly turn your face into the wind.

PART FOUR

RETURN

There
Eve and Judassa
I have enclosed them
like an ancient pod.

Corollary.

Trinity.

And despite all this
despite the odds
I have survived

and will claim this for ours
the reception female.

Prodigality
profligacy of seed

but I am the cave.

All descend and rise.

In the history of things

I am not often noted
but somehow in all of this
I am still there

still keeping some hearth warm
while the sky sings like a cauldron.

Perhaps the war goes on forever

and we are the ones
going on
after the event
filling the spaces
bringing life on a plate
waiting for the fire to pass
for the men to come home
for the child to be born.

And when the dry plain
is burned
and will not yield
and when the earth wrinkles and cracks
and the gates are closed against us
and the children die in our arms
and we think the dust has dried our tears forever

In my dancing and singing

you saw angels and devils
and still you did not find me.

I learned to live in some underground place
smiling
performing small favours.

I have been bought and sold
at ten years old
into the same old game

stolen moments, food, love.

Caught
invented baubles to distract you.

Fall on my back.
Offer my throat.

I am the old stock

the old tree

broken, twisted
but still there
holding on
fierce as a tiger
in the sun and bright air.

Once I was sensuous as a cat
and followed the light
in tender dance with sun.
You think I did not cry out
to feel limbs thicken
turn to wood.

I am reaped over
harvested for years
left fallow
gone to weeds.

Have given all with the carelessness of children.

The dry face of the glacier

cracks and screams
but
milky, silken waterfall
forgives
rushes to meet and fall.

I can rip through the patience of sediments
I can snap you like sticks.

I am ash and rage
and boiling rock

then return
thoughts
smooth as stones
laid on the river bed
in the honeyed laziness of summer.

We are tidal
seasonal
turning
returning
breaking away
washing over
dying
beginning.

Time flies in out of windows

like swallows building and leaving.

Dangerous empathy.

The season closes
like hands
like tears
and we are filled with it
slipping away from our arms
sliding into the ground

thoughts of leaving and never returning
tears to do with holding and leaving

the ageless tears of women.

Waiting for angels
you thought an answer had to come.

There is none.
And it is morning.

Thunder dins under a milk white sky

rain slants across the hill
drifts in the garden like ghosts.

The fire is in ashes.

The wild outside my window
is brambles, roses gone to briar
a garden without strength
blown, rambled, gone to weeds.
Will she return?

Will I return
wake again, build again
leaf upon leaf, light among leaves
swell pod, shed seeds in showers.

(I am generous to a fault
fickle, sentimental, full of clichés
debauched with bees in Spring
too gaudy for my age, you say, with flowers.)

Will I wake again

take a peach from a tree
touch The Hand
that kissed the world extraordinary

the spark that lit the sun, that gilt the moon.

❧ BOOK TWO ❧

MAP READING

After Adam died,
what the Sleeping Beauty saw

MAP READING

CONTENTS

PART ONE

CONDITIONAL SURRENDER

After Adam died
it haunted her

the memory of him

still loving him despite everything

(and him never saying what happened)

(About the tree)

The roses that he grew
in a garden green and ordered
now outside her window

and under her lapel, a leaden sea.

Whoever we offended by our act

and who has not been
in the last two thousand years or so

the body sacred like an old, old instrument
still plays the same old song

waiting for the darkness

overwhelming

I fall against you
I fall before you

warm-blooded
my skin is silken gold.

Through courtyards with veils I beguile you.

Don't you know when we touch
I go weak at the knees.

Biological imperative.

Choirs of sirens
and you tie yourself to a pole.

What the Sleeping Beauty saw

Perhaps I began in mirrors once upon a time.

Back then my sweet unattainable lady's favour
was enclosed in towers and forests
and knights
with chivalric grails in mind
and a keyhole eye at the door.

Did my tears heal the eyes of the poor blind prince?

The Beast - I married him remember, happily ever
after.

Jag on the mouths of horses.
Cruel second besting.
(The beastings are the Mother's milk after all)

Stadium of eyes.
Female Grotesque of Carnival
stone centre of my heart.

You see how easily you can get lost.

One hundred years of dust falls from my castle walls.

In those days they burned them as witches.

At the edge of the dark forest

At the edge of the dark forest
and the path has made itself.

Fear at the base of us

born with that scream

slither to cold earth.

What hands?
What arms?
What face?

What love
can ever be enough?

The One About the Birth

I entered into other realms
of pain and fear
and blood and death

fought in a kind of war
with a kind of heroism

became of mystery.
Germinal.

Night held its breath and you were born.

I heard your cry
saw your eyes scattering light.

We are wound into one
three but one
small unit on this earth.

You whimper in my arms
all the hurts of this great world
on your little shoulders.

The Knife and Abraham

(i)

She heard him go out
heard him take the knife
look for bindings
the boy muttering sleepily against him

and the thought
could not be believed

a child to be sacrificed.

A fire in a bush
a lamb

to set the scene for yet another death

required

between two thieves
and nailed to a tree

the mother and the women weeping
and hopeless.

(ii)

There was to be no more dying for causes
no more sacrificial offerings
to gods of love or war

no more believing in death

the true carcass swaying

after the dogs have given up.

(iii)

Wise and foolish virgins
trim lamps carefully
pass down dance lines endlessly

sing softly as if happily
handkerchief on hand.

Toss through the symbols
dance card and fan

butterknives – the diagonals.

Conditional Surrender
1 - Open Season

(i)

The Sleeping Beauty
was not networking
just slept through the hard bits
and there it all was lucky bitch.

Invisibility factors aside
Miss Havisham just had to sit it out.

In dinner sets
in spatial arrangements
behind glass doors
she may be dust-free

but afraid

of the woman with the lute
of symbols entrancing
rooms full of roses.

Snake at my shoulder sings.

(ii)

Waiting in queues
taking deadness for patience

waiting for miracles
keeping film on hand

pausing for excesses
(motel technic
spare and bare
hand luggage only
and a neat double glazing of the heart)

There the heart
can and will
move into sunsets

bullet of gold
move into heart
implode with soft fracture.

(iii)
Still the check-out girls
Check-check-check out my dreams.

I am no Persephone
would not do
for a long journey involving sacrifice

more Ismene
obedient
the follower of codes
with the white heart and destroying soul.

(iv)
In shock for years
after the purity of war
I see you
suddenly complicate the dance
(bee imagery
osmosis etc.)

"Goodnight" said the little concierge
"and God bless you."

"So sweet" said the young girl of the bird
"So sweet."

(v)
Goodbye and the fluttering of hands
goodbye and the fluttering of mouths.

Night can call a different tune
I am soft wing.

After dreams
leaning over the edge
I trail my hand though ice.

Conditional Surrender
2 - At the Pomegranate Gate

(i)
By the lamp's discerning I am found
prompt
feathers slightly askew.

Under dry implacable minds I lie wooden as a
catechism
still trying to mend the great divide
(stitches under my hair)

I rule lines: joyful discord fearful order
fearful discord joyful order
damned if you do
damned if you don't
play around with fire etc.
let sleeping dogs lie etc. etc. etc.

Drink tea and forget the blade sings.

The palace gate is open and I want to look at shoes.

News at seven dark at six.
Press the moment to its cliché.

Exit. Piano delicate.

(ii)

At Seven Years Young

At seven years young
the man in black
lead me to the dark box
where I whispered my desire.

Water for forgiveness
but quantum physics me
into an eternity
of seeking the licentious
with hot house intentions.

Armies of good wives agree
the Primrose Way
kept us on our backs and knees
for a higher purpose

waiting to be transfigured
waiting to be accused.

This new brutality is old.

(iii)

Forever Mardi Gras

Retreating for years
I turned suddenly
and saw you
Harlequin on a bicycle.

Have missed the circus crowd
the paper hoop

exotic collage.

Have tried many disguises.

I'm good at costume
the quick change emotion
tricks
sleight of hand.

Make a set
shift a scene
drop the curtain.

Still illusion
the mainstay of deities
(music, candles, incense etc.)

(iv)

Keeping House

She wondered
if like trees
the bad years showed

the cigarette and coffee years
the all-nighters.

And returning
out of context like a new broom
putting the kettle on
taking it off again.

Bare minimum and hard as nails

we ripped through it all like flowers.

(v)

Point to Life

The beauty of rain on leaves

all in the perceiving
of the mind behind
and the state of the heart
and the day.

The pale lamps of flowers
might bring you back

the wash of sea on your feet
can shock you
shake you with shells and thoughts of time.

A truth can roar and sing like waves
and bowl you over
shouting and laughing

drenched
and trying to stand
holding your hat down

and still there is more.

(vi)

Epicentral

I was running for the edge
when you caught me

was rescued into warm seas
subtropical in a dry wooden light.

Cicadas rev me up

send me raking over
old year resolutions.

Summer moves me
reptilian

out from under a rock.

(vii)

Reliquary

I from scissors and a tower
a briar rose
found somewhere between pity and treachery
caught somewhere between hands and wings …

Winter's indelible stencil
and we are come
barefoot

choosing carefully
words
looks
meanings.

All unnecessary.

"I was afraid I had broken your heart" she said
believing all things irreversible

all others
as unforgiving
as herself.

PART TWO

MAP READING

There are those
who take readings by the moon

plot courses
with the sea full in their faces

know that silver sharks
fly beneath

sense with the urgency of the duck's flight at evening
with the sadness of the black swan's calling.

I myself have missed whole rainbows
rushing to put on
sensible outdoor shoes.

Pty Ltd

Cleaning the copper bottoms
I am thinking of you
and all the more necessary work to be done.

Self-actualising in the supermarket
I transcend shelf after shelf
of unnecessary things to buy.

(This self I shelved yesterday
reappeared this morning
bright as a button
so I thought I might as well wear it.)

Woman after Postmodernist Reconstruction

The newest master dresses well
and speaks with virtuosity.
Dionysus in snow white shorts
breaks several records locally.

Woman as campstool squats and groans
pressed into service in the mall
takes courses to improve her mind
in preparation for the Fall.

Archetypal models pose
pivot on hind legs and stare.
Samson reads the morning news
while young Delilah grows her hair.

Features at times upon the couch
velvet queen on velvet pink
minutely recounts peccadillos
to her understanding shrink.

Extracts her shame with pincer points
gently with a moving blade.
Emotion flutters like a fan
use no hooks, design to fade.

Laughs and cries in equal parts
hears the constellation's power
decides to take the Primrose way
absolution by warm shower.

In the Alhambra coffee shop
writes verses out in common time
and missing all complexities
goes sailing down the Byzantine.

Making Beds and Lying

Gingerbread houses
don't fool me
I must make my own way
but still follow small signs
(white stones, bird song).

Working without wires
may set you free
or may ensnare.
Must trust
(only) the hands, the rhythm
believe in the act.

Cannot separate my history
from the space in the bed where I lay
and the skin of the pomegranate there on the plate.

Some cut clean of objects
I tumble in
lost in the stuff of families' past
blurring the boundaries
where I begin and end
where they begin and end.

Old rings
echo and bind.
Lamps
lace cloths
lovely

but somehow
someone else's life
impresses softly
(remember me
do not forget me)

and we cannot move
but they come too

taking the past with us
and adding our own.

Is this a journey to or from?

Dress Rehearsal Spring 5 am

I'm always getting ready
(for some dreamtime?)
always practising away
preparing an item
learning another step
collecting costumes
just in case.

Base sounds of the cricket and the frog
underscore me

thrush thrills her performance daily.

It is already dawn
already today.

Venus lingers softly
can return, return, return

(reminds)

for my limited season only.

The Passion of the Grebe

Even her name is ugly.

After the speckled wood ducks
the black swans
the pencil drawings of pelicans
she is small and dark and plain.

She inhabits this place
arrives shrieking and flapping
from the reedy bank
pushing them down
her small silver children
flip
disappear.

I am yet new in imagining
still draw weapons from my mind
blades of thought
the dry dust of cynicism
scrabble for scraps of knowledge
marvel at time's passing
say I am with you
but cannot act.

She moves like wind on water
rushing, bright, clear.

I am still between seasons
cannot believe
in the generosity of summer.
Turning the garden's sluggish clods
I whine and falter.

In Spring
half-leaved
fear the wind turning
the sap rising.

I walk again
the lonely line of hill.
Approach the safety fence.

Watch her
dive

then dreaming circles
on the dark mirror of the dam.

The Soldiers and the Girls

In Spring in France
there are white flowers
in the woods
like snow

and the first green leaves
are like a breath
among the delicate veins of winter trees.

Under these white crosses
lie twenty thousand men.

How do you see us
walking in the sky above you?

How does it seem to you now
through the dark earth of your quiet underground?

We are moved by an idea
bright as a jewel
"to die that others might live"

but suspect the hand that sent you
Gloria Pro Patria
and blew your face off

and wrote upon your cross
"No Mother's hand to close his eyes"
and, "Gone from my heart"

you
Unknown Soldier,
you should reach out of the ground,
hold onto our arms.

We drink wine
with fine white bread
while you are drowning in mud.

April / May / South

Winter comes early to this southern place
already the leaves are yellowing
(sometimes it's hard to distinguish
between Autumn and dying).

I could rent a corner of a white veranda
glassed in from the west wind
and the banks of grey cloud
sun-locked, a book waiting.
I could ride north to that place again
with the mangrove trees and red hibiscus
and old worn shells.

But part of me is already wintering here.
Like mosses along paths, on bricks
like the cold, new grasses preparing for the season
so am I.

On shorter, yellowing afternoons
I play with the dog throwing and returning a ball.
On shorter, yellowing afternoons
with blackening shadows
the woman plays with the tamed animal
throwing and returning a ball.

I fold my arms like a small spider
and wait.

At the Restaurant

The bread waiter has precise cues
to enter
with a selection of four breads
moments after
a starched white serviette
spreads across your lap.

Dishes and platters
arrive from a warm cloud
piano and girl mingle divinely
waiter forever renews romance
polishes glasses, refreshes flowers, lights candles.
But then … when you're dining
and falling in love
you need that waiter
to be attentive
delicate
discrete
as you touch fingers
and the singer sings
"It had to be you…"

"It's a fictional representation…"
"…a small section of…"
"Have you read…?"

Public Transports

You must be paranoid
if you think
that everyone stops talking
when you get on.

In the soft hush
of morning bodies…

The talk dangles
and returns
the tram moves off.

"I looked in at… yesterday
and saw those rings…
You could buy some for me…
…anytime…"

"Why?"

"Because you love me"

"…those shares…"
"…this price…"
"…that meal…"

In the soft crush
of human bodies…

```
FOR  A  JOURNEY  OF  UP  TO  TWO
SECTIONS  ON  ONE  ROUTE  THIS
TICKET   MUST   BE   SHOWN   ON
DEMAND  OR  ANOTHER  FARE  PAID
— NOT TRANSFERABLE —
```

The conductor's
hand on mine
with change.

How soft
the touch of human skin.

The Common Sense -To Nurses

Stumbling against sunlight
(like some patched butterfly)
I move off carefully, woodenly
on new (simpler for now)
flight paths from hospital carapace.

I am brought out of darkness
anchored in light again
by the ministration of hands.

This true divinity
humans
bathing another human
caressing the head of another
holding another.
Humankind.

Here is the midnight stable
the Samaritan's hostel
though no chorus of voices proclaims.

Night torches cut across the darkness
approach my misery
speak to pain.

They are the earth angels.

Human Being(s)

Where do I begin and end?

Where once the mailbox stopped at the curb
retained, defined
(right at the very edge of things)

now

(at the bridge crossing, the waterfall, an attitude of
trees)

the track to your house
the geography of bodies
the gap across the table
the distance between fingertips

eyes are glittering pools
dissolve in sleep.

A photograph to have and hold
one shot perfect.

Sun pours down shoulders.
I'm jealous of your very shadow.

Traffic roars like the sea.
Global mail arrives minutely.
I follow you on unseen wires
around corners, around worlds.

But you are Mercury
quick like an idea moving from mouth to mouth
breathing, panting in air
eyes for hunting at night
a too rich mix.

Where is the edge of us?

So many names in the phonebook like leaves
so many faces remembered.
(There they are waving in old home movies).

Shop fronts and shop dummy dreaming
lies at the ready, tantalize with new shapes
mysterious for a moment, like racehorse names.

Mirror mirror, pretty pretty.

Approximations, improvisations
covering tracks.

Look, break, shout. unleash.
Shake like a wet dog in the stench of seaweed.

Eyes watch the skies
clouds before the moon.

I find I've learned you off by heart.

When the sun breaks through
the leaves tilt.

Time's slow turtle towards the West
skies begin to clear

you and me up the apple tree
playing the morning by ear.

Dusty with Brown

You think you know me. I do not know myself.
I train quickly, keep easily within boundaries
am slow, solid, set.

You think you have me
can hold me

I shed conversations like skins.

Watch me
drop behind
slink sideways, slide away
throw back my head and scent the wind

slip through the trees
plunge into shadows
descend
devour
no discretion or delicacy
greedy eyes gleaming.

Meet me on a later road
(head down, friendly, slow wagging)

replete with secrets.

Bridge to the Four-Cornered Sea

Without you
rushing to the land's edge

to simplify to nothing
the ash of other days

without you
to re-start with gulls and sky
replace with mist
and the forever wash of sea sand

I am a country without a dance.

She the Moon

She the moon
she the sea
she the ship and country.

Between that long last sob
of tide-in and tide-out sigh
moon rises on sea.

Daring to be happy
I dance a few steps
at the sound of your small feet
chattering along behind me.

Can you hear my song?

Umbilical chord of voice.
The language mind
sanctifies hearth
centre of fire.

Night's dredging dark I hold you in my arms.

The hidden secret world is still
sweet tangent to the moon.

Bright new bronze penny of a moon.

❧ BOOK THREE ❧

TIES THAT BIND

*The martyrdom and resurrection
of Lindy Chamberlain*

At the heart of Australia in 1980, at Uluru, then Ayers Rock, a dingo took the Chamberlains' baby daughter. Lindy Chamberlain was accused of killing her baby and after two inquests was sentenced to life imprisonment without parole. Another baby daughter born while she was in jail, was taken from her. After three years in prison and a Royal Commission, the Chamberlains' convictions were quashed. But it was not until 2012 that a third and final inquest established that a dingo-dog had taken Lindy Chamberlain's baby.

How does she proceed – I wonder?

I imagine her being reborn "without baggage," as though a plant, the seed from the hand of Demeter, a Fertility Goddess in another story. In that story Demeter must search for her daughter Persephone who goes to the Underworld in Winter and returns to her mother in Spring – an explanation of the Seasons. Lindy Chamberlain "finds" another way of living, explaining, reclaiming herself from the prison of words that has become her story – in a city somewhere, not in Australia.

Mother of the Dog

(i)

Strange
how we can never (feel we)
deserve that look of worship.

Dear
down to the wire dogs
dear
such soft spirits

with teeth and stink.

(ii)
Thought she would make a good dog
(be one that is
in another life say)

all that begging for favours
tone of sympathetic understanding
through eyes and softest ears and wagging tail
and wondering about mirrors.

Leave a pile of bones at the entrance to the
Underworld.

At least it's always warm.

The Blackbird of Doubt

The blackbird of doubt
sits on my shoulder
and will not move.

They have taken my dimensions
stepped out in heavy boots

pegged down my possibilities.

Will I still look out
eyes gleaming
like children

into that last hour of light
ready for night flight.

Oblique - the flaw

Apollo the sun the eye of the bull
looks at you
fierce and full of power

is the eye of the god in another story
looking from the depths
bringing fires from darkness . . .

The children sacrificed in fires . . .

Oedipus to be pinned out on a mountain
eaten by wolves to prevent the story . . .

Abraham would have slit your throat you know
but just in time. . .

They say I killed you.
They want to crucify me

New Atlas Old Geography

(i)

Another blue and burnished day.

Under this arc of sky
the rock glistens.

Angles of light
still reach back to the dawn and the dark

and the trees
restless with the slightest air
and the grass whispering.

Enter this stage
sun brimming with its own purpose
into a new meridian

sure- footed once
but now become my naught degree

my nothing

this centre.

(ii)

Time even from the start
had its own beginning here
and another compass altogether

but still
at this place of Dreaming
myths and legends must mix and tumble
falling flailing down down under
coalesce
divide
impose.

And then like an accent
from another land
that cannot be removed
from the new language

two thousand years
and beasts of burden
carrying gifts for kings
another child . . .
two hundred years
and eyes wincing against the glare and flies.

The darkness still follows
the signs shift like sand.

Goes Without Saying
{ The Sorry Eve }

There I am casting shadows
she said

always always

like a garden of shadows
and the sunlight rolling through

failing to see
in the middle distance

the tree
the sun through
and a green glade

and the serpent
ascending.

There I am casting shadows
she said

always.

Persephone

I have adapted to changes in landscape
this underground
among the smooth stones
along the deep dark river.

Where does the light come from?
The entrance was long ago
and many months till Spring.

Persephone and Pluto

At least the story was clear cut.

There she'd be waiting for the sun to go
for the colours to change for the sky to darken
to sink into the earth with him

and even every last farewell
"It's all the same" he'd say and laugh
Living and dying it's all the same"
Commit to earth? You are the earth
and Spring will prove me right.

Blood Money Same Old Moon

You thought you'd buried me but you were wrong.

Three years of Ministry – I'll try to see it that way
with the dogs waiting.
The eagles never touched me.

In the interest of certainty
who am I now?

now linked to darkness
by your rustlings and searchings
and delving into murky bleakness.

The power of the word
yours against mine.

Tear and feed.
Grotesque.
Strip to the bone.

You lie down
to moulder and gilt with stench.

The Land Spoke. The Desert Spoke

The land spoke the desert spoke
to the people who belong there

lead me again and again in my mind
along a trail a marking they could see

to the last sign of her

to where the wildness took her

to where I touched the wild.

I dare follow her no further
but now I have no fear
she lead me to the truth
and (wanting to hold, wanting to be held)
I'm holding onto this -it's all I have.

I can never stay yet keep returning

to that desert place
sands grasses trees.
Embrace them like an eagle on the wind
against forgetting.

A Kind of Death

I grieve but have no tears
I am bound and frozen
turned to stone

and this is not darkness
but a glare of lights
of cameras and your eyes.

Gardens suddenly translate
to whispering suburbs and the street
and voices, billboards
evening news

witness
know me
mirror me.

One-way reflection
and nowhere else to go.

(Where will the I go of the eye?
only the black and endless night).

If I am queen of anything
no one wants my crown.

New Life and A Fine Distinction

(i)

A kind and unkind equation.

A house a home a cardboard box
no rooming in for you my darling child.

No trail of stones to bring you back
the sky is raining tears.

And all the tears of all the children
all the faces, eyes of sorrow
fill the night and fill the spaces
taken from our arms.

Who will wait and watch with me?
Will you watch all night with me?
I fear the dark will close me in
I can't recall her face.

I cannot shift the symbols, change the end.

A cup a table and a chair.

I am the disassembled weeping woman
dislocated here.

(ii)

How to live
I do not live
but study day by day
to hide
improve

this nothing of despair.

This desert is my everywhere
the dancing fires, stories, songs
leap and gesture in the dust
but even rhythms and the dust
cannot reach me here.

Now the cell-like cell descends
four walls all I want and need
secret as a spider here
spin the myth of all these days.

Only the moon
emblem of emotion

the shadows silent shift
the leaves lift
in momentary shudder.

Dreaming for My Child
Once at the Sea's Edge

(I)

There was a moment when
waiting for the waves to leave that tiny craft
he held one end and seemed to play and tug
then then play again
and the waves with him

as if having loved to hold him
sad to let him go.

There was that moment when
who held who played
the huge sea and the man
who struggled who played
all was one
or like another shape a third.

He was not given back
so willingly to the sea's edge
to the land's edge
as if he and the sea and the boat and the sand
for that moment became one

then with sweep of arm and shoulder
took the boat and turned towards the hill.

(ii)

I am withdrawing like a final tide
not quite a war zone
not quite an ending

work only on forgetting
voices, faces, needs, desires
(forget even concluding rituals
once vital signs
hung up like a coat).

And now I will not seek perfection
want
chinks, cracks, flaws, imperfection

the framing
smaller and smaller

till I am a footnote

a reference point

only one of many stories.

Talk-Back with Houseplants

Into this landscape one dimensional

strange
resume the rhythm of a house.

Labour saving devices
available to me

robotic.

Spring
can you wait

the leaves again
after the winter
and the green of hope.

Will I always also see

red sands
feel waves of heat
a burning sun.

At a Window Looking Out

(i)

At a window looking out

felt she could

dissolve
in joy.
Knowing there is also the door.

A wondrous treasure

of a window
and a tracery of cloud.

(ii)

On a river

begin aslant
under a streaming sky

after the morning and the pelicans
and cicadas rising and rising like waves
over the midday arch
under the huge old gums

and clear blue

and there

the small tent
fragile
but a certainty

and amen like a prayer
the fall of the willow's curtain.

So much beauty it will break your heart.

The rush of birds
feeding and falling through air
the dragonflies.

Feel the sun
dredging through flesh and bone
to sand and stone.

And mercurial again the evening
the light spiralling along water

the sudden birds rising
fill the sky.

Not Home Yet

I am flung up on the bank
gasping for air
you think you have me in the bag
that you can take me piece by piece.

Once you thought
I existed on paper only

only ever guessing

but guess what
you're snatching at straws
I'm already gone.

I'm hard-wired now
I'm brand new.

I was an empty well
waiting for the break

learned to live from sayings on calendars
(you'd taken everything else except the time)

Sacrificial you thought I was.
You turned me out like a dog.

The Game-show Host

And how will you rise from your prison utterly
changed and are you? the possibility of resurrection
of redemption a return of any kind quite out of the
question had never occurred to you you never
thought to ask assumed the worst all those stories all
those lies all things to all people and nothing left the
accusations laying blame prison would be easier cells
and divisions still feel the stinging claws of shame the
prodigal son the hunger for meaning the longing for
certainty no matter what the hell the terror of
children the prisoners an apprehension an
understanding all at once gestalt all those ballads all
those voices knew a thing or two face as mask no
fixed viewpoint watched by photographs of the
unblinking dead

come down come down from your ivory tower

hear the cheering hear the games room shout

He She You I We

(i)

And suddenly something slams shut like a vault
and she's flying along

shouting above the ghosts

along freeways and by-ways
in sheer disorder.

(ii)

I've seen you on highway signs

distances to you

mileages, times

a definite compass.

Everything points me
in your direction.

Second Coming

(I)

DEMETER

Finger of crone
down furrow
press seed to earth.

And the rains when they come
some kind of sacred when you plant and yield

though the darkness still follows.

And you think you can touch it
the rim of something felt not seen

the almost.

The voice keeps calling
laughing, half breathless
keep coming, keep coming
like music a street away.

No thought who leads or follows.

(ii)

BEAUTIFUL WEATHER
THE TRAVELLING SOUL

Coming up through layers of earth
feeling the roots reach down

(eyes and ears are sheathed against the sand and grit
the grazes on my face might show for a while
but cannot be helped
my hands are tied).

To say I have come further than such a one
or not as far as another

has become joyfully pointless.

I am born safely thus
keeping out of trouble from the start this time.

This second chancing

is shaken free of symbols
no glancing imagery.

The dry pod rattles its seeds.

Like Sun Worship

I'm designing you
studying you
I'm devouring you like a new city
all the maps laid out
buying the local news
marking the places

watching every aspect of you
mere souvenirs will never be enough.

All of you
the sudden breath of the underground
the freezing arc of snow

the low growl in your throat
as I approach
bowing your head
breaking away from my eyes.

Be careful

you bring me to my knees
land at your feet
like sun worship.

Burning Bright

You hook me out by the neck you know
with your jazz chords
you're too much of a good thing.

You have confused me utterly with delight.
I'm lost in an early dawn
like Venice in a mist.

I'm entranced, I'm inspired
I'm writing opera
and we are already on stage taking shape.

You will be soft and lamplight gold
forgiving (and I need a lot of that).

My time is now she said
I feel the life ascending
I feel the light descending
find you rising.

Running for Cover

The rain falls
pauses
roars
falls on us from a midnight sky.

We are running for cover
falling and laughing
dancing and shouting.

I am laughing and losing
and starting again
arriving and leaving
arriving again

all evidence
waiting like a photograph.

This morning we woke the dogs.

Chance and the Underground

Strange
how the walls, the buildings
evolve in place.

A cold rush of stars.

The wildness in your eyes
now only hinted at
replete.

And you're letting in a neon dawn
the traffic sounds rising
the weary pavement waiting for your step.

You heard the sirens howl in the night
like wolves
knowing everything, knowing too much
blurring the lines.

The subway holds us close.

Riding this underworld
crowded in
we stand and trust.

Finders Keepers

And even if you don't exist
even if I only dream you

there'll be those
who'll want to take you
keep you.

I will be wary
bee keeping with veil and smoke

finding the sweetness
knowing how to take it.

How do bees do it?

Some old chemistry there.

Uses of Fire

You have engaged my heart
wild sister self
with your soft talk.

You're wilder than me, she said
smiling and smiling.

And I answered,
I've only tip-toed
across a tiny corner of your estate
but I remember everything you said
and I'll draw a crackling circle
round this place
and I'm at the centre
fierce and on guard

like a cat mother

like a dog
hauling off bones to the world under.

No one can take me now.

Travelling Light. At the Sunset Inn

(i)

After a dead and blank horizon

I am at the edge
(keep going)

heart beating wings beating

heart beating
not breaking

watching the sky
hearing the thunder move along ridges

adjusting to the nearer landscape
within me
hearing at last the one call
within me

finding at last the well
full to the brim
surround me with your stories
bring me news.

(ii)

Safe now this is the time
the crickets suddenly singing
from cupboards
from under the mat

the brown butterfly days and yellow of late summer.

Morning sun warms like a cat
rolls like a ball across the floor
stops at your feet.

Down the hall is the door to the balcony
the door to the sunset
the view across the street
to the sand dunes and the sea.

I'm content
and need so little now.

I am preparing
watching the sky
over an inland harbour
preparing
to sail over an inland sea.

Grateful Acknowledgements

To Elaine Hutton and the late Greg Smith for insisting that I should read Mary Daly's Gyn/Ecology

To Kristin Henry, Judith Rodriguez, Sister Veronica Brady, Paul Collins, Brian Edwards, Kim Powers, and the members of Imago Writers and Ibis Writers for reading and commenting, for their conversations and their encouragement;

To Heather Murray Tobias for insisting that I should contact Littlefox Press;

To Jane Matta Ford for her inspiring and beautiful artwork;

To Christine Mathieu and her Littlefox Press for all her enthusiasm and dedication to the production of this book.

To Leigh Milne for saying: "to be born again instead of born of woman"

And to Russell and Tom

The following poems were first published in:

1994: Map Reading in New Zealand Poetry Society, *the old moon and so on.*
1997: The Soldiers and the Girls, Pty Ltd, Bridge to the Four Cornered Sea in Ibis Writers Anthology *A Skein of Ibis.*
1998: Dusty with Brown, Passion of the Grebe, Woman after Post Modernist Reconstruction in Ibis Writers Anthology *A Skein of Ibis.*
2002: Conditional Surrender 2 At the Pomegranate Gate in Box Hill Institute Anthology *Inkshed 13.*
2002: Mother and Child, The First Labour was Hers, In the History of Things, I am the Old Stock, in Poetica Christi Press Anthology *Mother Lode.*
2003: Mother and Child proposed as part of a liturgy on Motherhood and the Sacred Conference, Golding Centre for the Study of Women's History, Theology and Spirituality.
2004: Change Room, Public Baths, in Poetica Christi Press Anthology *Set Free.*
2007: After Adam Died, Wise and Foolish Virgins, In the History of Things, in final edition of Woman Church *An Australian Journal of Feminist Studies in Religion.*
2012: Human Being(s) placed first in Artists' Society of Phillip Island *Figure it Now* poetry competition.

Previous work by Petrea Savige

Return the Garden a book of poetry, Nosukumo 1983.

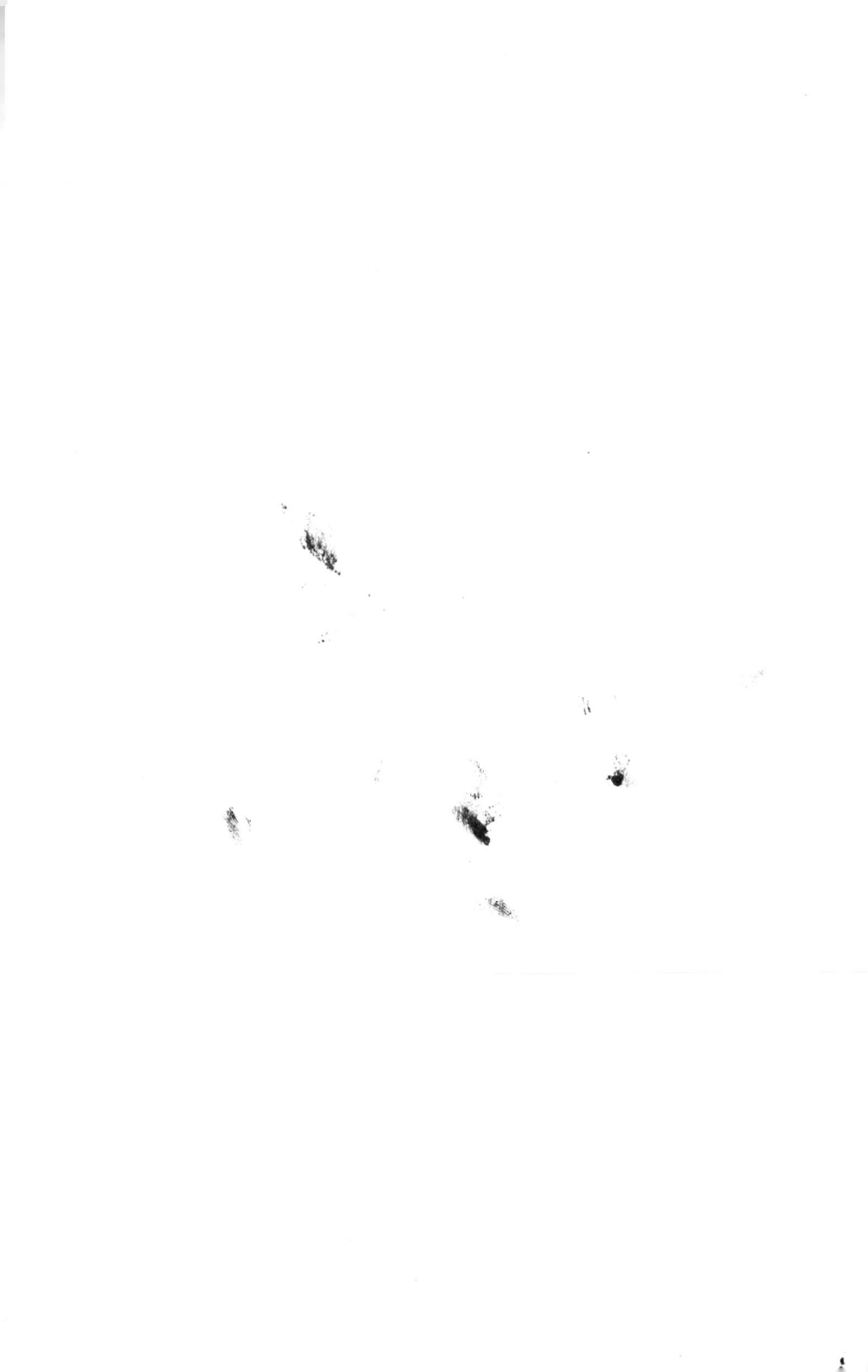